Michel de Verteuil CSSp

YOUR WORD IS A
LIGHT FOR MY STEPS

Lectio Divina

They glorify the Lord at work in themselves.
The Rule of St Benedict

Pray for. Sr. Brid. RSC

VERITAS

Published 1996 by
Veritas Publications
7-8 Lower Abbey Street
Dublin 1

Reprinted 1997, 1998

ISBN 1 85390 376 0

British Library Cataloguing
in Publication Data.
A catalogue record for
this book is available
from the British Library.

Cover design by Lucia Happel
Printed in the Republic of Ireland by Paceprint Ltd, Dublin

INTRODUCTION

I would like to introduce you to the ancient method of Bible reading called *lectio divina*. It is a method which has borne much fruit in the Church through the centuries but which has been neglected in recent times. Today it is making an important contribution to Church renewal.

Lectio divina is practised in the Bible itself but was given the name and systematised as a method in the fourth and fifth centuries. For the first thousand years of the Church it was the most common way of reading the Bible. It is still the way we pray the Bible in the Prayer of the Church and the liturgical year is based on it.

This method of Bible reading is based on six principles:

1. *Lectio divina* is a dialogue between the written biblical word and life experience. In a dialogue our experience throws light on the Bible word, bringing it to life for us so that we feel at home with it. The Bible word in turn throws light on our experience which is thus transformed from merely being an event to being a word of God spoken to us.

2. *Lectio divina* presupposes that every Bible text speaks to the imagination. It invites us to enter through our imagination into the movement of a Bible passage, discovering that this is the movement of our own lives too.

3. In *lectio divina* we discover a double story of sin and grace, first in the Bible and then in our individual lives, in the history of every community and of humanity itself.

4. *Lectio divina* is different from most Bible-reading methods in that it is an exercise both of theology and of prayer: of prayer in that we respond to the exercise of sin and grace in our lives; of theology in that we gain a new insight into the workings of sin and grace

in our lives and in the lives of others. Through *lectio divina* we grow in awareness and we pray, awareness leading to prayer and prayer leading to awareness.

5. Another thing that makes *lectio divina* different from other Bible-reading methods is that it can be done by all, irrespective of educational background. Even illiterate people can do it. Whatever our educational background, we must humble ourselves before the Bible text so that we can really listen to it. We can all, by reflecting on experience, make this text come alive.

6. *Lectio divina* requires both personal freedom and the sense of community. Our encounter with the text must be personal. No one can dictate how or why it touches us; to do good *lectio* we must trust our own feelings. On the other hand we must not read the Bible in isolation, but allow our personal response to resonate with others, a community, if possible, and if not, at least one other person. So, too, we must regularly enter into the insights of others. In this respect *lectio divina* is quite different from what used to be called 'private interpretation'.

In the early days *lectio divina* was a systematic and disciplined method both of prayer and of theology. Today it is often presented purely as a prayer method but in fact, it is especially as a theological method that *lectio divina* has an important contribution to make to the Church today.

THEOLOGY

Let us first clarify what theology is. This is important because one of the problems with theology today is that it has lost its specific character.

The classical definition of theology, formulated by St Anselm in the twelfth century, is *fides quaerens intellectum* – faith seeking understanding. Theology therefore presupposes faith. Having come to faith we try to express it a systematic and coherent way.

As theology develops, it gradually gives birth to doctrine. Faith then comes to be expressed in clear formulations, three persons in one God, two natures in Jesus, and so on. Doctrine is the fruit of theology but cannot replace it.

Through theology our faith becomes dynamic, gives meaning to life, provides a vision for the future. It must be done systematically, so that it is coherent, can be explained and handed on to others, can make sense of the whole of life.

Through theology, also, our faith can be expressed in the language of our culture. When theology is not alive, our faith loses touch with culture, and is no longer a dynamic force in society. This is a constant danger for the Church and has, in fact, happened to a large extent. We have compartmentalised our faith so that it no longer addresses the pressing concerns of humanity. A return to *lectio divina* can help us address this problem.

Let us take a brief, and necessarily over-simplified, look at the history of theology.

TWO KINDS OF THEOLOGY

We can distinguish two kinds of theology in the history of the Church – 'community' and 'school'.

'Community theology' has been called 'monastic' because as time went on it was practised mainly in monasteries. However this is really a misnomer, giving the impression that it was a method for celibate men, living apart from the secular world. This was an accidental development; what was essential was that it was done in a life-community – a parish (or diocesan see) – more often than a monastery.

'School theology', on the other hand, was practised in the universities which developed especially from the eleventh and twelfth centuries onwards.

These two theologies followed very different methods, each determined by the setting. Whereas the setting for school theology was the classroom, that for community theology was the liturgy, especially the weekly Eucharist, and the homilies.

School theology was practised by an academic elite, community theology by the whole Church community. School theology used reason and objective analysis. Community theology was creative, used imagination and feelings, song, dance, poetry and painting. School theology created its own language and culture, understood only by those who practised it. Community theology was integrated into the local pre-Christian culture – its feasts like Christmas and Candlemas, its artists and thinkers: Plato, Aristotle, Cicero, Virgil, Catullus.

Up to the eighth century, community theology prevailed in the Church. From then on, and especially from the eleventh century, school or scholastic (as it came to be known) theology took over and has been dominant ever since.

The Church will always need school theology but it must be complemented by community theology. We can identify three problems with theology today which make it imperative that community theology – and *lectio divina* which is its most important form – be given its rightful place in the life of the Church.

THEOLOGY FOR A WORLD CHURCH

According to the famous German theologian, Karl Rahner, we can, with some over-simplification, divide the history of the Church into three periods – the Jewish, the Greco-Roman and the universal.

The first group of the followers of Jesus saw themselves as a renewal movement within the Jewish faith. They had no idea that they were starting a totally new religious group.

Gradually non-Jewish converts began to join in ever-greater numbers, bringing their own language, culture and philosophy. It was the beginning of the second period, the Greek Church, which eventually became Greco-Roman and then European.

As the New Testament texts testify, the transition to this new era was painful, marked by dissension and much bitterness.

According to Rahner this period lasted until our own century. We are now in the third period – a world Church, in which all the cultures of the world must come to feel at home.

This cannot happen in theology, however, for the simple reason that the theological method which has become dominant in the Church does not come naturally to those of non-western cultures.

Non-western people are always at a disadvantage

when they do theology. They do not lack wisdom or discipline; the problem is that they cannot master its language or thought-patterns. They are not therefore making their proper contribution to the theology of the Church.

The same can be said for many people in the west. To do theology demands money, time, an academic background. Ninety per cent of people are thus excluded. Like non-western people, they are always at a disadvantage and must be content to receive the crumbs that fall from the table of the elite.

A world Church needs another theological method where all can feel at home. *Lectio divina* is such a method.

THEOLOGY AND PRACTICE

A second need is to rediscover theology as a practical science: much theology today has little or no bearing on our social situation.

This is a serious abdication of responsibility. As the present pope often reminds us, we Christians are called to play our part in building a new kind of civilisation. To do that we need a theology, which is nourished by and leading to involvement in the secular world.

It is interesting to note that some modern governments have recognised the revolutionary potential of theology.

The Reagan administration in the 1980s, for example, found it necessary as part of the political strategy for Latin America to focus on liberation theology as a threat to US plans for the region.

The South African theologian, Fr Albert Nolan, was once asked whether he regretted not being directly involved in the struggle against apartheid. 'I am directly involved', he said, 'through the subversive activity of theology.'

Lectio divina is that kind of theology, deeply subversive of all forms of oppression.

THEOLOGY AND SPIRITUALITY

Theology has equally little bearing on spiritual growth. The two have been put into separate compartments. Spiritual directors regularly warn seminarians and others who study theology that they must do so with caution. Theology, they say, tends to make people proud and therefore must be supplemented by (perhaps even curbed by) spiritual reading and prayer. Great theologians are seldom canonised nowadays.

This compartmentalisation was unheard of when community theology prevailed. Theology was spiritual reading, it often went hand-in-hand with mystical experiences. Both theology and spirituality have suffered from being kept separate. *Lectio divina* brings them together again.

THE METHOD

The name
Lectio divina is best translated as 'sacred reading', reading as a sacred exercise, one that draws us closer to God. It is a reading not only of the Bible, but of experience; we discover the Bible in our life-experiences and we find our life-experiences in the Bible, each helping us to understand the other.

Through *lectio divina,* the Bible becomes a living book and the events of life become words of God.

NEED FOR DISCIPLINE

In our western world, the terms 'disciplined' and 'popular' are often considered to be in opposition. We take it for granted that disciplined study of the Bible is only for people who have had formal education. People say, 'I like to work with simple people because they have such beautiful insights into the Bible.'

But who are 'simple' people? We are all complex beings, prejudiced and inclined to see things from our own points of view. Some people have formal education, others have very little or none, but for all of us 'simplicity' is something we must strive after and this requires discipline. In any case it is untrue that people without formal education cannot study in a systematic, disciplined way.

They must of course have a method which they can master, but popular theology is in fact systematic, deep and coherent, as it must be to merit the name of theology.

THE DISCIPLINE OF THE STORY

To understand *lectio divina*, we must distinguish two kinds of reading: textbook and story. By textbooks I mean anything we read for information, including the daily paper and the broadcast news. Nowadays stories are told not merely in books but on radio and television.

In textbooks we are looking for facts that are objective and static; our reason is active. In reading stories, something different is happening. There is movement in a story and we enter into the movement by identifying with the characters; our imaginations are active, our feelings and emotions get involved; we are not objective but subjective.

A common error in our culture is that we read (or listen to) textbooks for learning, and stories for entertainment. Textbooks, we say, are serious, stories are not. Adults, we believe, learn from textbooks, children (or 'primitive people') from stories. People say that the Bible tells stories because the Jews were not as sophisticated as we are.

All this is totally untrue. Stories are much more serious and important than textbooks. In our culture, as in all others, they are the most powerful, indeed the only way to communicate values. Parents tell their children stories about life when they were young; how, though wealthy now, they were once poor; how, though poor now, they were once well-off. They do this not to entertain but to communicate their values, self-worth, respect for those less successful than ourselves, hard work.

Tribes, nations and religious groups all hand down their traditional values in the same way, not in textbooks but by stories, songs, statues and paintings.

Textbooks teach directly, presenting facts. Stories teach indirectly; we identify with people in the story and spontaneously take on their values. This, by the way, poses a problem today when it is thought that stories are purely entertaining. We do not realise the values we are picking up. Because the people are attractive we gradually begin to think that their racism, violence and sexual irresponsibility are not so bad.

What about the Bible? Is it a textbook or a story? When asked the question, many say textbook, others a mixture of story and textbook; very few say, spontaneously at any rate, that it is a story. This is because of our idea that stories are not serious.

In fact, there can be no doubt at all. The Bible is a story, the story of God's people. We can sum it up as the story of Jesus, prefigured in the Old Testament, told in the gospels and lived again in the New Testament Church.

The Bible contains different kinds of books; apart from stories in the strict sense there are also histories, proverbs, poems and laws. But they were all meant to be read as stories, for readers to enter them and so adopt their values.

The ancients took this for granted but today it is difficult to get it across. People have been taught that wisdom can be taught through reason. Even non-European cultures, where story-telling is so much part of the tradition, have been made to feel that it is an inferior way of communicating.

God knows human nature however, and he taught us the deep lessons of life through stories – individual stories and the one great story of Jesus. If we are to learn in the way he taught us we need to re-educate ourselves in the art of storytelling.

Saying that we tell a story says nothing one way or the other about whether what we say happened historically or not. What it says is that we are using a certain form of communication. This clarification is very important for bible reading. The Bible contains many different kinds of writing, some of which are the accounts of historical events. All, however, use the kind of communication we can call story. *Lectio divina* is story-reading of the Bible.

HOMECOMING READING

There are two kinds of story-reading: **alienating** and **homecoming**.

In alienating reading, we identify with the characters but remain foreigners to them. The world of the story is not ours; we are alien to it.

Television soap operas are a good example. Once we switch off the TV, it comes home to us that our world is not the world of the little screen. The characters in that world are more exciting and romantic than we are, not merely because of their clothes, homes and cars but also because of their conflicts and triumphs. This is, in fact, the attraction of the soaps; they offer an escape from the drab world in which we live.

This is especially so in many deprived communities today where, through satellite TV, people living in dire poverty can watch not merely shows but advertisements for things totally outside their reach. These are stories that they cannot possibly enter and which give no meaning to their lives – alienating reading.

Homecoming stories are totally different. They are the stories parents tell their children to help them understand themselves, 'we are respectable people', 'we have worked hard', 'our house may not be as nice as the neighbours' but we can be proud of what we have achieved.'

Similarly, the stories of saints or national heroes enable us to understand where we have come from, where we are going, why we are the way we are.

Are Bible stories homecoming or alienating? Let us take, for example, the central story of the Israelites' passage through the Red Sea. The Israelites are fleeing, fearful of the Egyptians pursuing them; they come to the sea, itself a fearful place with its great monsters. Moses puts forth his wand and parts the waters, the Israelites walk through in safety, to freedom.

Tell a group that story, in all its drama, and ask them, have you ever had an experience like that? They will always answer, 'No, nothing so dramatic has ever happened to me.' But that's not true. We have all had the experience of feeling cornered, danger behind and before; then somehow God brought us through and we gained a new freedom.

The trouble is that we are accustomed to a Hollywood-style presentation of the story, stressing the marvellous, so that it becomes a unique event which happened in times past, in some faraway land, to extraordinary people.

The Bible, therefore, can be read as an alienating story, but it was not meant to be so. It is a homecoming story, and in *lectio divina* we read it that way, discovering in it our stories and the stories of people who have touched our lives.

Our constant diet of alienating stories has it ingrained in us that our life stories are not worth celebrating, that the Bible is alienating too. But the Bible was written to tell us who we are, not merely who we should be or will become. Through *lectio divina* we become conscious that we are sacred stories, a consecrated nation, a priestly people.

LECTIO DIVINA IN THE BIBLE

Let us listen to a passage from Isaiah, which shows clearly that the method of *lectio divina* (not the name) is practised in the Bible itself.

'Thus says the Lord, who makes a way in the sea, a path in the mighty waters, who brings out chariot and horse, army and warrior; they lie down, they cannot rise, they are extinguished, quenched like a wick. Do not remember the former things, or consider the things of old. I am about to do a new thing; now it springs forth, do you not perceive it? I will make a way in the wilderness and rivers in the desert. The wild animals will honour me, the jackals and the ostriches; for I give water in the wilderness, rivers in the desert, give drink to my chosen people, the people whom I formed for myself so that they might declare my praise.' (*Isaiah 43:16-21*)

These words were written at a time when the Jews were in exile in Babylon. They had been a great and powerful nation but, mainly because of their internal divisions, were weakened and became vulnerable to neighbouring powers. They were invaded, defeated in battle and sent into exile. As exiles, they were exploited and forced to do menial work; a people proud of their past history now deeply humiliated.

We do not know if Isaiah was himself a member of the community in exile or if he was one of those who remained behind in Palestine and came to Babylon as a missionary. In either case, he is giving the people a Bible teaching and does it in three movements:

1. First he tells them the old story of the Exodus. He does it as a good storyteller, dramatically, speaking to the imagination, and not too concerned about being historically exact.

Let us imagine the people listening. There must have

15

been different reactions, some cynical: 'What has this story got to do with us?', others escapist and nostalgic: 'What a beautiful story! Just what we needed to make us forget our present difficulties!'

2. Isaiah anticipates both reactions: 'I am not talking about the past.' He has told the old story not to make them cynical or escapist, but for them to recognise that God is doing a similar deed in their own time. He doesn't tell them what should happen, or what will happen if they behave themselves, but what is actually happening. 'I am doing a new thing, now it springs forth, do you not perceive it?' This is *lectio divina,* telling an old story and then discovering that it is really a story of the present.

3. Isaiah then does an interesting thing: he goes back to the old story and the biblical language, he speaks of rivers in the desert'. This is the journey of Bible reading, we start with a passage, discover it in life-experience and then go back to the passage, now read as our story. The passage is now ours, we find ourselves in it. Isaiah goes further. The old story becomes more wonderful, glorious, the new exodus more glorious than the first one; it is at the same time a promise for the future, water from the rock will become a flowing river, wild beasts, jackals and ostriches bow will down before God's people. Again, there is no moralising. Isaiah is showing the people how to interpret their lives, and in a perspective of hope.

Here then is *lectio divina* as practised by Isaiah. We too can read the Bible text, see it come alive in the present, and become a promise for the future. These are not different readings but one, the Word of God in the Bible text in the present and a potential for the future.

Isaiah is a model of the theologian – a biblical storyteller, able to tell the old story in such a way that the hear-

16

ers recognise themselves and feel secure in it. This is why theologians (and preachers) must know not only the Bible, but what is happening in people's lives today.

Isaiah also shows us that Bible teaching must not be reduced to moral exhortation as it usually is today. Of course there are moral conclusions to be drawn from *lectio divina*, but as with all story-reading these flow spontaneously from the reading. We don't have to harp on them; like Isaiah we may not need to mention them at all.

THE THREE STEPS

The method of *lectio divina* is very simple. There are three steps: **reading, meditation** and **prayer**. All must follow the discipline of the steps, university graduates as well as those with only primary education, doctors of theology and those who have never followed a Bible course.

Even those who cannot read or write can do *lectio*. In the early monasteries, only a few monks could read but the whole community did *lectio divina*. Someone who could, read the text for the others, explained it to them and then left them to meditate and pray on their own, at work or in the Church. The same thing is happening today in poor communities, and this is a lesson about God being 'no respecter of persons' when he speaks his word.

The setting can be anywhere, a church if convenient, if not, a simple hall, a home; it does not have to be secluded, children can be running around outside, or sleeping on their mothers' laps. There is no need for expensive equipment, overhead projectors or audio-visuals. If there is no electricity, candles will do; the only things necessary are the Bible and people of faith.

The second and third steps of meditation and prayer especially can be done anywhere, in the bus on the way to work, doing the dishes, watching the children play, on the beach – a lesson, too, of how God speaks to us through the events of daily life and how we can live continuously in his presence.

Reading

Two things happen at this stage. First we familiarise ourselves with the text, let the words sink in and reverberate within us (or in the group if we are doing it in common). People sometimes speak as if Catholics don't set much store on the words of the Bible. To distance us from the fundamentalists they say that we focus not on the words of the text but on its meaning.

This is not our position. The magisterium has several times rejected the opinion that inspiration covers only the meaning and not the words of the Bible. The constant tradition of our Church is to give great importance to the words of the Bible. In the liturgy the text is proclaimed with great reverence, incensed and accompanied with lights. According to an old custom, those who say the prayer of the Church must move their lips as they pronounce the words.

Lectio divina is traditional, therefore, in starting with a slow, reverential reading of a text. We read it several times, omitting nothing and remaining open to being touched by any part of it. On the other hand we discipline ourselves not to add anything, to guess what Jesus might have said or done, apart from what is in the text. Our entire focus is on the text before us.

At this stage we are also situating the text, in its historical context first – Old or New Testament, a stage in the history of God's people, the life of Jesus, the young Church; then in its literary context – history, poetry, parable, proverb. Some background from a teacher or a written commentary may be helpful.

We will usually have to divide the text, unravelling it so that we can be open to the particular section which in time will touch us. All this is part of 'reading' and after a while we will find ourselves moving to the next stage.

Meditation

'Meditation' in *lectio divina* is different from what the term means in other prayer methods: we enter the passage, we 'recognise' it. Our imaginations, and especially our memories, are active.

We recognise one of our role models in Jesus when he says, you must take up your cross and follow in my footsteps, a dear friend in Mary accepting to play her part in her son's work of salvation, a hesitant member of our youth group in the rich young man.

Sometimes this will take time. We wonder what is the point of the parable of the useless servant; then after meditating for a while we gradually recognise our parents, giving themselves to the service of their children when they come home from school and content to eat when they have all been served. Jesus calling St Peter 'Satan' reminds us of the touching moment when we recognised that in trying to protect someone we were really preventing them fulfil their vocation.

Prayer

Spontaneously we find that meditation leads us to prayer. If it has been a healthy meditation, our prayer will take three forms: thanksgiving, humility and petition, not necessarily in that order. Humility and petition usually come easily; thanksgiving does not, so we must make sure that it is part of our prayer. What we are thanking God for is that he has 'done a new thing' in our lives, that Jesus is alive among us. If we do not find ourselves thanking it means that we have not 'recognised' the passage and we must go back and complete the meditation.

Then comes a crucial moment in the *lectio*: we move from praying in our own words to praying in the words of the passage. Instead of saying 'Thank you, Lord, for this person who has been an inspiration to me', we say 'Thank you for this Jesus who said that unless I take up my cross and follow in his footsteps I am not worthy of him.' Not, 'Thank you for that friend who accepted to play his part in my life', but 'who said, I am the servant of the Lord, let it be done according to your word.'

This will be awkward at first, but in time will come spontaneously. What it means is that we are now going back to reading, and the cycle will start again; it will lead to deeper meditation and then to deeper prayer.

Lectio divina is therefore an ongoing reading of the Bible and of experience, not a start-and-stop activity, but an attitude, a way of life. We are fulfiling St Paul's command 'never to stop praying'.

Deepening the meditation
Sometimes people ask, 'Will I be able to find myself in this passage?' In *lectio divina*, that question is not asked. We approach the passage in the faith that God wrote this passage for us, as a homecoming story, so that we are certainly in it. The only question is whether we will open ourselves to meeting him there.

We can go further and say that every Bible passage cannot merely touch us but can do so very deeply. Much of our reading remains on the surface both of the passage and of ourselves. When we have done a good *lectio*, however, we have the feeling that the passage was written especially for us and that our whole lives are in it.

One problem with getting there is time and another is method.

A *lectio* will be deep only if we give it several days, struggle with the passage, work our way through various interpretations, follow one path, then another and then a third. The traditional practice of the Church is to spend a week on a passage and my experience is that it is a good rhythm. If we have plenty of leisure, while on retreat for example, we may be able to go a little faster. We must also deepen our *lectio* by remaining faithful to the method. We repeat the three steps, going deeper each time. One memory comes to us and leads us to prayer, then when we come round again another memory comes, this time more intimate and touching, then a third and so on. Some Jesus we had forgotten who came to our lives at a crucial moment and transformed us, perhaps saved us from a pharisee who almost destroyed our self-confidence for ever. A deep peace comes over us. We are moved to tears, beyond the joy, sadness or regret, we have a double feeling of very great gratitude and humility.

Deepening also moves towards communion with other people, 'Jesuses' close to us and far away, faces of him that we have seen on our television screens, or read about in history books, our personal saints. We meet our fellow sinners too, Pharisees and rich young men, minor sinners and also the great evil-doers of history, not self-righteously, but conscious that we share in some way in their sinfulness.

Throughout we remain at the level of feeling, true to the text and to life experience.

THE MOMENT OF WISDOM

As we continue our meditation we begin to be aware of behaviour patterns, in us and in others. We find we are saying not merely, this happened to me (or to someone else), but, this has been a constant pattern in my life, and then in the lives of other people who have touched my life.

We become conscious that 'this always happens', life is like this: all good people act like Jesus, all mean people like the Pharisees, all oppressors like Pharaoh; this is how God always acts. This is the moment of insight, what we can call the wisdom moment of *lectio divina*.

We have neglected the wisdom aspect of Bible reading (it is of course neglected in our culture generally; 'Where is the wisdom we have lost in the knowledge?', T.S. Eliot wrote). But wisdom is given great importance in the Bible itself; Solomon prayed for wisdom as the greatest of all gifts, and St Paul often prayed that his communities would be blessed with wisdom.

We have turned Jesus' teaching into moral commands but in fact it is mostly wisdom teaching, 'the kingdom of God is like this ...', 'the first will be last and the last first', 'he who loses his life will find it'.

Every bible reading should lead to wisdom. It doesn't, for the same two reasons: we don't give ourselves sufficient time and we don't have a good method.

We should not stop our meditation until we come to the wisdom moment and recognise and welcome it. If we follow the method we will find that the insight we come to has certain characteristics.

First, it is expressed in a statement; not one applicable to Catholics only, 'going to Mass is very important', or 'Jesus is really present in the Eucharist', but universal so that we could share it with a group of Hindus or

Muslims or even unbelievers. It is therefore an insight that has implications for society.

It is wisdom of the heart, the fruit of meditation, not of reasoning, an unexpected gift that we receive with humility and celebrate, not something that is imposed on us, from outside or even from our wills.

The wisdom moment is not the time for moral exhortation, far less command, although moral consequences are implied in the insight. We don't have to spell out these consequences (as we have seen, Isaiah didn't and Jesus often didn't either) but we know they are there and without saying so we commit ourselves to implementing them.

The insight always strikes us as new, or at least with new clarity, so that we experience it as a call for repentance and we spontaneously pray for forgiveness that we hadn't seen it before. Since it has social implications, a critique of society is implied: it is 'subversive'.

The wisdom moment is not static; very spontaneously we move back to prayer. Only this time the prayer is more contemplative.

LECTIO DIVINA AND CONTEMPLATION

Some writers make contemplation a fourth step in *lectio divina*. This is not the tradition however, and I don't think it is right. All prayer must be in some way contemplative so we should never put prayer and contemplation into separate categories. It is better to say that the prayer is in two stages, differentiated and undifferentiated (or contemplative) prayer.

As we have seen, meditation leads to thanksgiving, humility and petition. These are different kinds of prayer, and we know which one we are saying. We can call this differentiated prayer. If, however, we stay with the passage long enough, we find that our prayer gradually becomes simple, and in two ways.

First, we find that we merely repeat the words, without differentiating between the three kinds of prayer. If someone asked us if we were making a thanksgiving on a petition, we couldn't say; we are doing both together.

Secondly, we find that we are using fewer and fewer words of the passage, 'get behind me Satan', 'forgive them', 'revealed them to little children'. After another while, we are saying the words with our hearts, not saying them – our lips do not move – and yet saying them.

We can call this the contemplative moment of *lectio divina*. A moment because, as with the wisdom moment we can identify it, welcome it, speak about it. It is contemplative because we are not active, merely resting peacefully in the truth of the passage – which has become through meditation the truth of ourselves. We must stress that contemplation is an inherent part of *lectio divina*; *lectio* is always meant to go that far. It is opposed to the notion that contemplation is reserved to those who live in quiet surroundings, or withdrawn from the world.
All are called to share in the banquet, the mother with six or seven children in a two-room house, the working man whose only time for meditation is on the way to work. The only thing necessary – the wedding garment – is the humility to wait for the Lord.

The contemplative moment also brings out the great limitations of moralising reading, which is so common today. In moralising the passage tells us what is wrong with us and the conclusion is that we should put this right or at least ask God to put it right. We cannot rest in the passage. With *lectio,* on the contrary, we can, because, we discover God at work in the world, and this is the deepest truth of ourselves and of all creation.

INTEGRATING PRAYER

Lectio divina is not merely a method of Bible reading; it is a way of life, based on a certain understanding of God, the Church, ourselves spiritual growth.

Through *lectio* we can understand why the Church became the kind of Church it is – Catholic in the sense of whole and integrated.

Over the past few centuries it has become the custom to divide theology into areas – dogma, moral, ascetic, and so on. This undoubtedly has its value, but the danger is that theology will lose wholeness. Done through *lectio divina* it is one, unified meditation on the word of God, integrated into liturgy, personal and communal prayer, and the rhythms of our daily lives.

Through *lectio* we live continually in the presence of God at work in the world.

SAMPLES OF *LECTIO DIVINA* PRAYERS

THIRD SUNDAY
LUKE 24:13-35

JOURNEY TO WISDOM

Jesus leads the two disciples along the slow, painful journey to wisdom, and God is inviting you to remember with gratitude when he led you to understand life more deeply than you did. You may like to focus on Jesus as teacher, remembering who played that part for you.

The story unfolds itself in stages:

Verses 13-16: Identify with the disciples as they walk aimlessly, discouraged, not able to make sense of what has happened to them. Jesus is discreet, patient and content to walk with them.

Verses 18-24: Jesus invites the disciples to tell their story. It is significant that the story is long, with ups and downs, and that Jesus listens in silence.

Verses 25-27: Jesus only now takes up the dialogue; he shows that the teaching of the scriptures is not full or complete until it is experienced as being lived out in our lives. On the other hand, he shows the disciples that what had seemed senseless now appears not only meaningful, but in accordance with age-old laws of life.

Verses 28-32: What Jesus taught them on the road now becomes a reality in the context of a community meal.

Verses 33-35: A crucial part of the story: as a result of the encounter with Jesus and the growth to wisdom the disciples are able to return to their daily occupations with new heart.

PRAYER

Lord, there have been times when we were totally discouraged. We walked aimlessly along the road, our faces downcast, as we remembered the sad events of the previous days:
  - the project we thought would change our country;
  - a relationship that would fulfil all our longings;
  - a Church community that would be at last a true body of Christ.
All the while you walked with us even though we did not recognise you. You listened in silence as we told your story once more. Then, when the moment was right, you showed us how foolish we were, how slow to believe the full message of the prophets.

Now it was our turn to listen in silence as you explained the passages throughout the scriptures that were about ourselves, and our hearts burned within us. We remember with gratitude how we were able to set out that instant and return to Jerusalem.

Lord, our contemporaries are walking the road, their faces downcast, making no sense of their lives. Forgive us, Church people, that we come arrogantly to them:
  - calling them materialistic or addicts;
  - telling them our own story.
Help us rather to be like Jesus:

*- to walk with them in silence, so discreetly they don't
even know who we are;*
*- to ask them to relate their stories even if they are impa-
tient with our questions;*
`·` *- to listen respectfully for as long as the stories last.*
*How else will they be able to explain the scriptures at work
in their lives, so that they can return to Jerusalem, their
hearts burning within them?*

Lord, give us a deep understanding of the Bible:
*Send us teachers like Jesus who will make our hearts burn
within us as they talk to us on the road and explain the Bible
to us.*

*We thank you for those special Eucharists that we expe-
rience from time to time:*
- when we know that the Bible passages are about us;
*- when we recognise your presence in the breaking of
bread;*
*- when we feel no need to linger there, but return to our
daily occupations, our hearts burning within us.*

*Lord, we always want to grow in wisdom quickly and
painlessly, by doing courses or reading many books. But there
is no other way except to pass through times when we cannot
understand what has happened to us; only when we have
told our story many times over, experiencing again and again
how senseless it is, will we reach down into the roots of our
traditions, and discover with surprise that what we have
gone through is nothing new but the fulfilment of ancient
prophecies.*

*Lord, we get to know you through teachers and preachers
and we thank you for them.*
*But it is only in a community of sharing and trust that we
can really experience your presence in the world.*
How true it is that we recognise you in the breaking of bread.

SECOND SUNDAY
GENESIS 15:5-12;17-18

VOCATION

According to the constant teaching of the Bible and our long Christian spiritual tradition, when God calls men and women to fulfil some mission in the world he first gives them an overwhelming experience of his love, unconditional and irrevocable.

Knowing they are loved in this way is the foundation of their mission. As Jesus told the apostles, God does not want servants but friends. (John 15:15).

This crucial teaching on how God calls us for mission emerges from the stories of biblical characters like Isaiah, Ezekiel, the servant of the Lord, the Blessed Virgin Mary, St Peter and St Paul. Saints of the Church over the centuries have been called in the same way.

It is significant that in St Luke's account of the transfiguration which we read on this Sunday, Jesus in glory speaks with Elijah and Moses about *'the passing which he was to accomplish in Jerusalem'* (9:31).

This passage is a typical story of God calling, it is one of several accounts of God making his covenant with Abraham, or Abram as his name was then.

The covenant had two aspects, descendants (verses 5 and 6) and land (verse 18). Both required an extraordinary act of faith on Abraham's part; he was childless and already old, and he had no claim whatever on the land of Canaan he had come to. His trust must be based entirely on God's spoken word and the experience of his presence.

Each of us has received a personal vocation from God, one that we take stock of at times like Lent and on personal retreats.

Meditating on the story of Abraham is the opportunity to celebrate, for the first time or as a joyful memory, the moment when we knew that God called us, and also to renew our trust in his love.

PRAYER

Lord, we thank you that when you choose us human beings
to carry out some mission in the world
  - to be spouses, parents and friends,
  - to bear witness to Jesus in the world
  - to minister in your Church
  - to be men and women of prayer
you always start by giving us a deep experience of your love:
  - you took Abram outside and made a Covenant with him
  - the angel Gabriel called Mary 'full of grace'
  - the heavens opened for Jesus at his baptism
  - Jesus took Peter, John and James up to the mountain to pray
  - you conferred the stigmata on St Francis of Assisi
  - you revealed to St Thérèse of the Child Jesus that her mission in the world was to tell of your unconditional love
  - you inspired Pope John XXIII to convoke the general council of the Church
  - the founder of Alcoholics Anonymous had an experience of your healing power.
We too have had such experiences.
Sometimes you take us outside at night and make us feel connected to the whole of creation and to all humanity;
we look up to heaven and feel we can count all the stars because they are ours,
we imagine the millions of human beings who will come after us and know that they are our descendants,
we put our faith in you and know that you have for ever justified us.

At other times it is as if we have fallen into a deep sleep and terror has seized us.

At other times the cloud of your glory covers us in its shadow and a voice comes from the cloud that we are in the presence of your Beloved and must listen to him.

These are experiences so deep that when they are over we keep silence, like the three apostles, and tell no one what we have seen.

We are filled with awe like Abram when he had cut the animals in two and put them half on one side with the other half facing on the other.

And when the sun had set and darkness had fallen, there appeared a smoking furnace and a firebrand that went between the halves.

Ever afterwards we feel assured of your love: if at times we feel lost, we know that the whole world is our home, from the wadi of Egypt to the Great River; if at times we feel lonely and abandoned we know deep down that all men and women are brothers and sisters to us.

Thank you, Lord.

THIRD SUNDAY
EXODUS 3:1-8; 13-15

CONVERSION

The story of Moses' encounter with God in the burning bush can be read in different ways. It is itself a story of vocation which parallels last Sunday's account of Abraham's call. I am proposing that you meditate on it as a story of conversion.

According to the constant teaching of the Bible and our tradition, every deep experience of God is a conversion experience. Jesus reminded us of this when he said in this Sunday's gospel reading, *'unless you repent you will all likewise perish'* (13:3, 5) and also in his parable of the Pharisee and the Publican (18:9-14).

In the passage Moses, like ourselves when we meet God, experiences conversion in two directions. We would like to be in the presence of God and at the same time remain aloof from our brothers and sisters in need.

God led Moses (and he wants to do the same for us) to awareness that true humanity is never merely *'to be'*, even to be with God; it is always *'to be with'*.

The second stage in Moses' conversion is to renounce the desire to know God's name. In the Bible 'naming' means assuming authority over someone or something. This is the significance of Adam's naming of the animals in Genesis 2:19-20. God teaches Moses that he must be content merely to know that *'God is'*.

We too need this conversion, and repeatedly, as we constantly fall back into the basic error of wanting to take control of God. It is always one of our Lenten conversions.

PRAYER

Lord, Lent is a conversion time:
  - *some of us experience conversion in the course of our
    parish mission;*
  - *others when, after a long delay, we finally make up our
    minds to go confession;*
  - *for others again it just happens that for some mysterious
    reason, you give us a special call during this season.*
There are different levels to our conversion experiences.
Sometimes they are a radical turn around:
  - *after years of infidelity we return to spouse and family*
  - *we give up alcohol and drugs*
  - *we enter a seminary or religious community*
  - *we go back to church after a long absence*
  - *we adapt to serious illness*
  - *we accept that it is time to retire.*
At other times the conversion is less dramatic:
  - *we find that we can forgive someone*
  - *our prayer life becomes more contemplative*
  - *we start reaching out to someone at work.*
*However and whenever it happens, it is always a Moses expe-
rience and we celebrate now his story and ours.*

*Just as Moses with his flock of sheep wandered to the far
side of the wilderness, so we were drifting far from our roots,
with no direction to our lives, but without our knowing it
you had brought us to Horeb, your holy mountain, the place
where we would meet you in a totally new way and as if for
the first time.*

It all happened suddenly and quite unexpectedly:
  - *like Jacob when he wrestled with you at Bethel*
  - *like St Peter when he caught all the fish*
  - *like the woman who met Jesus at the well*
  - *like St Paul on the road to Damascus*
It was a scary feeling and we didn't quite understand what

was happening, all we knew was that something important was happening to us, that we should come no nearer, must take off our shoes because the place on which we stood was holy ground.

We were in your presence, the Father of Jesus, the God of Abraham, Isaac and Jacob and of our ancestors too.

For a few brief moments we thought we could just remain enjoying the feeling, but very quickly you made us see that you were calling us to conversion.

You hadn't called us to focus on yourself, what concerned you was the miserable state of your people in Egypt, the sound ringing in your ears was their appeal to be free of their slave-drivers; you were well aware of their suffering, and were totally committed to delivering them out of the hands of the Egyptians and bringing them out of that land to one that was rich and broad, a land where milk and honey flow. The reason you had brought us here was because we were the slave-drivers ourselves or at least did not share your concerns.

Lord, we knew we wanted to change but we felt so inadequate:
  - *what would we do?*
  - *wouldn't people sneer at us?*
  - *what authority did we have, when we and others knew us as sinners?*
  - *what could we say when people asked us who was sending us?*
  - *what were we to tell them?*

Then after a while we understood that we had a further conversion to make to complete trust.

  We were looking for security, we wanted to feel sure that our conversion was complete and irrevocable and that we would not fail again.

  But the final conversion is when we decide to move ahead, taking one day at a time, and leaving the future in your hands.

You are the Lord God of our fathers, the God of Abraham,

the God of Isaac, and the God of Jacob, the Father of Jesus,
and have really sent us,
but we cannot hold you as our possession.
All we know is that you are and we must be content with
that, this is your name for all time and for all generations.
Amen.

FOURTH SUNDAY
ACTS 13:14, 43-52

SUCCESS AND FAILURE

In this page we are far from Jerusalem. A gentile community has been set up in Antioch and this community has become missionary in turn. They commissioned Paul and Barnabas to go out and found new communities and their journey has taken them to the city of Antioch in Pisidia.

What happens here is typical of all times of growth. It also summarises the story of the Acts, fulfilling the story of Jesus. The message is preached first to the Jews who reject it; it is then preached to gentiles who receive it joyfully. This had been prophesied by Jesus: *'There will be weeping and grinding of teeth when you see Abraham and Isaac and Jacob and all the prophets in the kingdom of God and yourselves turned outside'* (14:28).

We are also reminded of Jesus' first preaching in Nazareth, (Luke 4:23-30). We have lived these two stories of grace and sin; sometimes we have done so when in God's plan we brought a saving word to others, at other times when we accepted or rejected a word ourselves. Our meditation will lead us to celebrate the experiences of grace and mourn for those of sin.

'Those destined for eternal life' (verse 48) is a significant designation of the Christian vocation, typical of Acts.

'Shaking the dust from their feet in defiance' (verse 51) was commanded by Jesus in Luke 6:5. We must interpret the gesture correctly. It cannot be an act of self-righteousness nor of condemnation since these are not permitted to the followers of Jesus; it expresses rather inner freedom by which they are able to move somewhere else and give themselves to others.

PRAYER

Lord, once we decide to widen the scope of our project we are sure to meet failure.

At first it is a small group of friends, we all know one another, share the same values, have similar goals.

From the time that, like Barnabas and Paul, we move out of familiar territory into the unknown and take our seats in the synagogue of Antioch in Pisidia, we find that some will not want to hear our message. We understand then the constant teaching of the Bible:

- *Jeremiah's vocation was to tear up and knock down.*
- *Mary said that to lift up the lowly you would have to cast the mighty down from their thrones.*
- *Simeon prophesied that the child was destined not merely for the rising but also for the fall of many in Israel.*
- *Jesus taught that even when disciples are repaid a hundred times over it is not without persecution.*

There is on the one hand the great satisfaction of knowing that we have brought light where there was darkness; that we

- *showed broken people that they could take decisions for themselves*
- *taught the illiterate to read and write*
- *helped sinners to experience your forgiveness*
- *reconciled warring groups in society.*

We experience that you have made us a light for nations so that your salvation might reach to the ends of the earth.

Many whom we have helped now come to talk with us and we urge them to remain faithful to the grace you have given them.

It makes them happy to hear this and they thank you for your wonderful message.

On the other hand, however, alongside all this success something else is going on — the rejection of the good news, people using blasphemies to contradict the truth, using their influ-

ence among the upper classes of Church or society, persuading them to expel your messengers from their territory.

Lord, if ever we respond with anger or discouragement, or go away with the dust of the city clinging to us, it is because we have forgotten that it is your work. Help us to shake the dust off our feet and move on to somewhere else, trusting that whatever good we have done remains, and those who profited from our work are filled with joy and the Holy Spirit.

NINETEENTH SUNDAY
MATTHEW 14:22-33

CALMING OF THE STORM

At first reading today's passage looks like one story but in fact there are several stories woven into it and it would be too complicated to meditate on them all. You must therefore separate the various strands and focus on one of them.

There is first of all the action of Jesus in sending away both the disciples and the crowds so that he could go up to the hills by himself and pray.

Then we have the dramatic story of the disciples in the boat, far out on the lake, clearly symbolical of ourselves in times of crisis. You can go straight to the climax of the story: Jesus gets into the boat and the wind drops so that they bow down before him.

You might like to focus on Jesus walking on the water. For the disciples the sea was a hostile element, containing terrifying monsters. Jesus walking on the sea, especially in a storm, is symbolic of his power over evil.

It significant that when the disciples saw Jesus they were terrified, thinking he was a ghost. Ask yourself what would make them respond like that.

The incident with St Peter is obviously added on to the main theme of the story. It has touched the imaginations of Christians over the centuries, has been painted many times, and has been the subject of countless sermons. Let it evoke some personal memories, either focusing on Jesus as the model leader or guide, or on St Peter as a model of ourselves when we take a bold step and then, once we have stepped out, are afraid.

PRAYERS

Lord, great leaders are like Jesus, They know that a time comes when they must be alone. They insist on leaving even their closest companions and the crowds they have nourished they send away so that they can go up to the hills by themselves to pray.

'Religion is often rejected as reactionary. Yet the Christian faith properly understood and wholeheartedly followed is a force for radical change and renewal' (Cardinal Hume, May 1990).

Lord, our civilisation is going through a great crisis.
We are like the apostles on a boat far from any shore,
battling with a heavy sea and facing a headwind.
There are people who want to take risks,
to try new ways of doing things and create alternative institutions.
They will know that the Church is really the presence of Jesus if they hear us calling them to leave the safety of the boat and step out even though it means walking on the water.
Lord, there are times when we feel so disillusioned that even when you come to us with power over evil:

- a friend whom we can trust;

- an invitation to a retreat;

- an opportunity to relaxation;

we think it is a ghost and cry out in fear.
Lord have mercy on us.

The moment we cease to hold each other,
the moment we break faith with one another,
the sea engulfs us and the light goes out'
(James Baldwin).

Lord, we thank you for faithful friends,
the kind that when we feel the force of the wind and take a
fright,
we only have to say, 'save me', and they put out their hands
at once and hold us.
Lord, prayer is experiencing that it is really you who are there
with us,
feeling the urge to go beyond our limitations and to hear you
say that we can do it,
then suddenly becoming aware of the risk we have taken and
feeling afraid and then knowing that you have put out your
hand and held us.
Thank you, Lord.
Lord, let Jesus be our model in our work of spiritual guid-
ance.
When we find that our charges have little faith, don't let us
become impatient or reject them;
help us rather to put out our hands at once and hold them.

> **'A young woman said to an old woman: What is life's**
> **heaviest burden? And the old woman said: To have**
> **nothing to carry' (A Jewish tale).**

Lord, we feel sorry for people who only know about giving
what they have left over.
They do not know the joy of giving everything they possess to
a cause they believe in.

THIRTY-THIRD SUNDAY
MARK 3: 24-32

END OF THE WORLD

This is the final teaching of Jesus' public ministry. The language is symbolic and through your meditation you will be able to enter it.

You can divide the passage into three sections. They are connected but since the language is so symbolic it is better to focus on only one at a time and let yourself be touched by it.

Verses 24 to 27 are a teaching not merely about the end of the world but about the 'end-of-the-world experiences' which individuals as well as communities go through from time to time.

Verses 28 and 29 are a parable of small signs of hope within a general atmosphere of winter. Identify with Jesus pointing out these signs.

Verse 30 gives urgency to the parable. It was a true prophecy in the time of Jesus. In what sense can we say that it is always true?

Verse 31 can stand by itself as a powerful statement of faith in the future. You can read it as a statement made by Jesus to us, or you might ask yourself to what extent Christians can speak with similar confidence about their own statements.

PRAYER

Lord, we remember with gratitude the crisis times in our lives:
- *a spouse proved unfaithful*
- *we lost our job*
- *we fell into a serious sin*
- *we learned that we were seriously ill.*

Our world fell apart in those days, after that time of distress. The sun was darkened, the moon lost its brightness, the stars came falling from heaven, and the great powers of heaven were shaken.

But you did not abandon us.

In the midst of all that turmoil we received a great grace:
- *we understood for the first time the meaning of faith*
- *we discovered inner resources we didn't know we had*
- *friends rallied round us.*

We experienced your saving power coming in the clouds with great power and glory and sending your angels to gather us, your chosen ones, who had been scattered to the four winds, from the ends of the world to the ends of heaven.

> *'The more solitary I am, the more affection I have for all my brothers' (Thomas Merton).*

Lord, when we are driven by our ego, we put people into categories,
- *rich and poor*
- *saved and sinners*
- *developed countries and developing world.*

When we enter into our nothingness before you, letting the stars we aspire to fall from heaven and the great powers be shaken, we experience your angels gathering together all those people whom, in our wilfulness, we had scattered to the four winds.

'If we listen attentively we shall hear amid the uproar of empires and nations a faint flutter of wings, a gentle stirring of life and hope' (Albert Camus).

Lord, we thank you for those people who, when everyone else sees only deep winter, perceive that the twigs of the fig tree have become supple, and that summer is therefore near, a new era is coming, is at the very gates, and that before this generation has passed away new and wonderful things will have taken place.

Lord, prayer is trusting totally in your love, knowing with unshakeable confidence that heaven and earth will certainly pass away but your love for us will not pass away.

Lord, the freedom which Jesus bequeathed to us enables us to do our best without having to worry about when or where it will bear fruit.

Like him, we are quite content to acknowledge that as regards the day and the hour of success, no one knows it, neither the angels of heaven, nor ourselves, no one but you, our loving Father.

'The dark period is over and Europe is on the threshold of a new era' (Pope John Paul II in Hungary, August 1991).

Lord, we thank you that we have seen stars fall from heaven and great powers shaken.

Your chosen ones who were scattered to the four winds are being gathered to build a new future.